# CAMBRIDGE

Greenman & the Magic Forest

STARTER

Marilyn Miller
Karen Elliott

CAMBRIDGE
UNIVERSITY PRESS

University Printing House, Cambridge CB2 8BS, United Kingdom

One Liberty Plaza, 20th Floor, New York, NY 10006, USA

477 Williamstown Road, Port Melbourne, VIC 3207, Australia

4843/24, 2nd Floor, Ansari Road, Daryaganj, Delhi – 110002, India

79 Anson Road, #06–04/06, Singapore 079906

José Abascal 56, 1º - 28003 Madrid, Spain

Cambridge University Press is part of the University of Cambridge.

It furthers the University's mission by disseminating knowledge in the pursuit of education, learning and research at the highest international levels of excellence.

www.cambridge.org
© Cambridge University Press 2015

This publication is in copyright. Subject to statutory exception and to the provisions of relevant collective licensing agreements, no reproduction of any part may take place without the written permission of Cambridge University Press.

First published 2015
20 19 18 17 16 15 14 13

Printed in Spain by Coyve
Legal deposit: M-3611-2015

ISBN	978-84-9036-814-5	Pupil's Book Starter (with Stickers and Pop-outs)
ISBN	978-84-9036-815-2	Big Book Starter
ISBN	978-84-9036-816-9	Teacher's Book Starter
ISBN	978-84-9036-817-6	Guía Didáctica Starter
ISBN	978-84-9036-818-3	Teacher's Resource Book Starter
ISBN	978-84-9036-820-6	Flashcards Starter
ISBN	978-84-9036-819-0	Phonics Flashcards Starter
ISBN	978-84-9036-821-3	Class Audio CDs Starter
ISBN	978-84-9036-822-0	Digital Forest Starter
ISBN	978-84-9036-845-9	Routine Board
ISBN	978-84-9036-000-2	Reward Stickers
ISBN	978-84-9036-001-9	Reward Stamp
ISBN	978-84-9036-846-6	Teacher's Bag
ISBN	978-84-9036-844-2	Puppet

Cambridge University Press has no responsibility for the persistence or accuracy of URLs for external or third-party Internet websites referred to in this publication, and does not guarantee that any content on such websites is, or will remain, accurate or appropriate.

Thanks and Acknowledgements

Authors' thanks

Marilyn Miller would like to thank everyone at Cambridge University Press and in particular to: Jeannine Bogaard for providing the opportunity to write, Julieta Hernández for overseeing the project and Mercedes López de Bergara for her excellent editorial skills and continued support.

Karen Elliott would like to thank everyone at Cambridge University Press and in particular Mercedes López de Bergara for her enthusiasm and dedication to the phonics section of the project; Mary Ockenden at the American School Bilbao, Aitziber Gutiérrez and Piluca Baselga at the Colegio Infantil Haurbaki for their help and suggestions on phonics at various stages of the project.

A special thank you goes to Juan González Cué, our Production Project Manager.

The authors and publishers would like to thank the following teachers for their help in reviewing the material and for the invaluable feedback they provided:

Álvaro Ruiz González, Colegio Ramón y Cajal, Madrid; Carlos B. Ferrer de las Peñas, Colegio Montpellier, Madrid; Paloma del Cerro Gómez, CEIPSO El Greco, Madrid; Miriam Martínez de Dios, Colegio La Anunciata, Madrid; María Palomo Bosque, Colegio San José, Madrid; Carmen García, Salesianos Atocha, Madrid; Gloria Torrecilla González, Colegio El Valle, Madrid; Cristina Álvarez, Colegio Ramón Gómez de la Serna, Madrid; Mª Jesús Aragón Rodríguez, CEIP Velázquez, Madrid; Leyre Alcalde Gordo, CEIP La Alameda, Madrid; Mª Cruz Salomon García, CEIP Infanta Leonor, Madrid; José Rubén Jiménez Carvajal, CEIP Seseña y Benavente, Madrid; Antonio Hernández García, Colegio Santa Joaquina de Vedruna de Sevilla, Sevilla; Sara Fernández Moratilla, Colegio Virgen del Carmen, Barcelona; Raúl Vercher Gómez, Colegio Sagrada Familia, Valencia; Joaquín Martínez Rueda, Colegio Narval, Murcia; Silvia Crespo Rica, Colegio Santo Tomás de Villanueva, Granada; Vanesa Rubio Carreño, CEIP La Pea, Valencia; Lidia Madroñal Vaquero, Colegio Santa Joaquina de Vedruna, Sevilla; María Del Mar Jiménez Calvillo, CEIP Las Cigüeñas, Madrid; María José Cortés Moreno, CEIP La Raza, Sevilla; Rosa Mª Montané Milà, ZER Cep de Sis, Barcelona; Raquel Lara Sánchez, Colegio La Milagrosa, Madrid; María José Pascual Núñez, CEIP Monte Alegre, Valencia; Inmaculada Folgado Aliaga, Colegio Asunción de Nuestra Señora, Valencia.

The authors and publishers acknowledge the following sources of copyright material and are grateful for the permissions granted. While every effort has been made, it has not always been possible to identify the sources of all the material used, or to trace all copyright holders. If any omissions are brought to our notice, we will be happy to include the appropriate acknowledgements on reprinting.

The authors and publishers would like to thank the following for permission to reproduce photographs (and materials):

p. 33(t): Shutterstock/© ChiccoDodiFC; p. 33(b): Shutterstock/© Breadmaker; p. 59 (t): Shutterstock © Piotr Marcinski; p. 59(b): Shutterstock/© Dasha Petrenko; p. 85 (t): Shutterstock/© Brykaylo Yuriy; p. 85(b): Shutterstock/© Adam Wasilewski; p. 95(t): Shutterstock /© Krsmanovic; p. 95(b): Shutterstock/© Sanchai Khudpin.

The authors and publishers are grateful to the following illustrators:

Gema García Ingelmo: cover illustration and characters concept
Antonio Cuesta Cornejo: illustration

The publishers are grateful to the following contributors:

Sarah Mc Connell: editorial freelance
Teresa del Arco: layout and design
Chefer: cover design
Riera Sound / Suena Estudio: composition, arrangements and audio production
Amy Jo Doherty: additional composition

Contents

Unit	Topic	Language	Phonics	Page
Routines		**Weather:** *sunny, cloudy, windy, raining/rainy, snowing/snowy, hot/cold.* **Shapes:** *circle, square, triangle, rectangle* **Numbers:** *1 – 4* **Colours:** *red, blue, green, yellow*		
Welcome Unit – The Magic Forest		*Greenman, Sam, Nico, Rabbit, Hedgehog, Frog, Stella; Hello, I'm (Sam). What's your name?*		**5**
Unit 1 – Let's Draw!	classroom	*teacher, table, chair, book, crayon, pencil; What's this? It's a (pencil). It's (red).* **Concepts:** *happy/sad* **Colours:** *red* **Shapes:** *circle* **Emotions:** *sad/happy* **Value:** *creativity*	*s (Stella)*	**9**
Unit 2 – Let's Play!	toys	*ball, teddy, doll, train, bike, car; There's one (blue) (train). Here you are. / Thank you.* **Concepts:** *fast/slow* **Colours:** *blue* **Numbers:** *1* **Emotions:** *excited* **Value:** *fun*	*g (Greenman, green)* *b (book, blue)*	**21**
Review 1: Autumn Fun!		**review:** *classroom and toys vocabulary*		**33**
Unit 3 – The Big Monster	face	*face, eye, ear, mouth, nose, hair; I can see one (big) (face). I can see two (big) (ears). It's got (one) (big) (mouth).* **Concepts:** *big/small* **Numbers:** *2* **Colour:** *green* **Emotions:** *fear* **Value:** *imagination*	*n (Nico, nose)* *m (mouth)*	**35**
Unit 4 – My Family	family	*mummy, daddy, brother, sister, baby, friend; Who is it? It's (Sam's) (brother). They look (the same). They've got (big) (eyes).* **Concepts:** *same/different* **Numbers:** *3* **Shapes:** *triangle* **Colour:** *yellow* **Emotions:** *curiosity* **Value:** *family*	*f (frog)* *u (umbrella)*	**47**
Winter Fun!		**review:** *face and family vocabulary*		**59**

Contents

Unit	Topic	Language	Phonics	Page
Unit 5 – Where's My Bird?	pets	turtle, fish, bird, hamster, cat, dog; Can you see your (bird)? It's (on) the table. The (cat) is (under) the (chair). **Concepts:** on/under **Numbers:** 4 **Shapes:** square **Emotions:** worried/relieved **Value:** helping	d (dog) c, k (cat, kitten)	**61**
Unit 6 – Let's Tidy Up!	food	sandwich, cake, pasta, apple, banana, milk; I like (milk). / I don't like (pasta). Let's (eat). **Concepts:** tidy/messy **Shapes:** rectangle **Emotion:** regret **Value:** being tidy	p (pasta)	**73**
Review 3: Spring Fun!		**review:** pets and food vocabulary		**85**
Festivals 1: Halloween		cat, monster, pumpkin	h (hedgehog) a (ant)	**87**
Festivals 2: Christmas		Christmas, tree, toy	r (rabbit, red)	**89**
Festival 3: Easter Carnival		Easter egg, bunny, chocolate	e (egg)	**91**
Festival 4: Green Day		forest, flower, beautiful	t (tree)	**93**
Review 4: Summer Fun!		**review:** course vocabulary		**95**

The Magic Forest

Name _____   5

Lesson 1

❋ What's your name?

❋ Welcome to the magic forest song: Listen and sing.

❋ Play the story.

❋ **WORKSHEET 1**: Say the names and colour.

Greenman and the magic forest

Welcome to the magic forest.
Adventure has begun!
Greenman and the magic forest.
English is such fun!

Let's go to the magic forest.
Adventure has begun!
Greenman and the magic forest.
English is such fun!

Greenman and the magic forest.
Adventure has begun!

❋ Optional: Colour the forest.

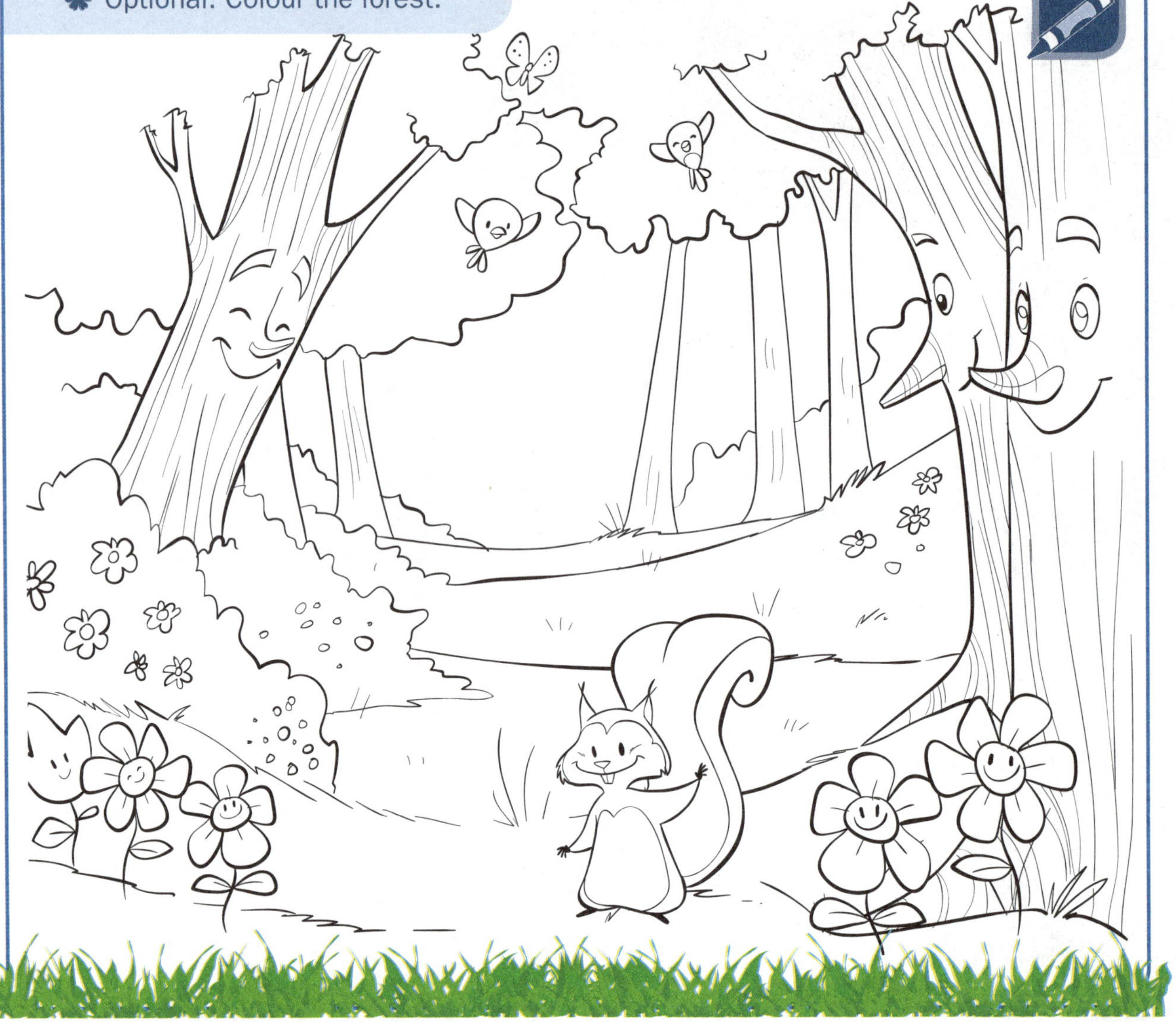

  Greenman, Sam, Nico, Rabbit, Hedgehog, Frog, Stella.
Hello, I'm (Sam). What's your name?

6

Lesson 2

❋ Meet the animals.

❋ Act it out.

❋ Play the story.

❋ **WORKSHEET 2**: Say the names and colour.

❋ Optional: Draw yourself in the playground.

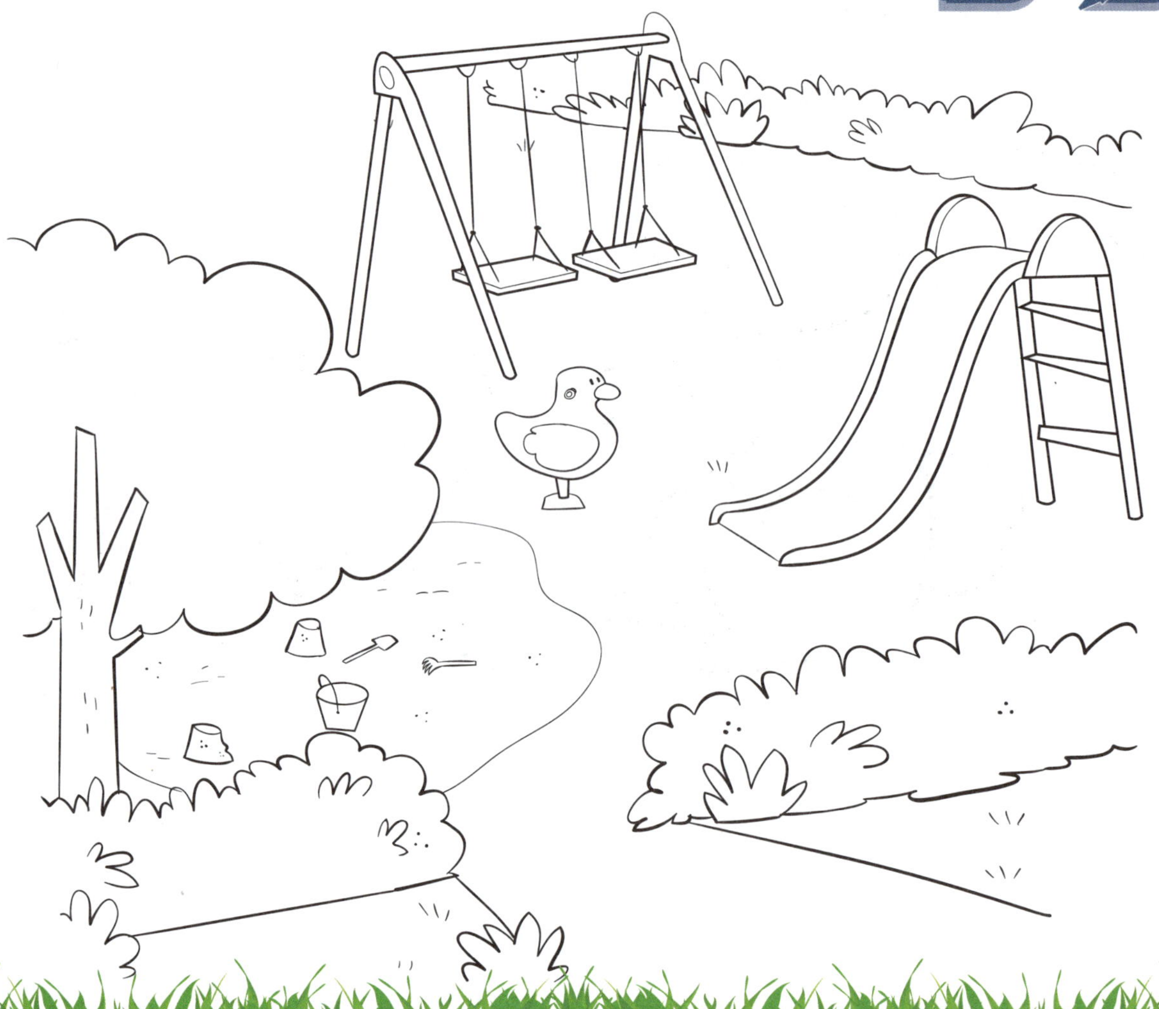

 Greenman, Sam, Nico, Rabbit, Hedgehog, Frog, Stella.
 Hello, I'm (Sam). What's your name?

1 Let's Draw!

Name

9

Lesson 1

❀ Help Greenman!

❀ *Hello, teacher!* song: Sing and point.

❀ **WORKSHEET 1:** Say and colour.

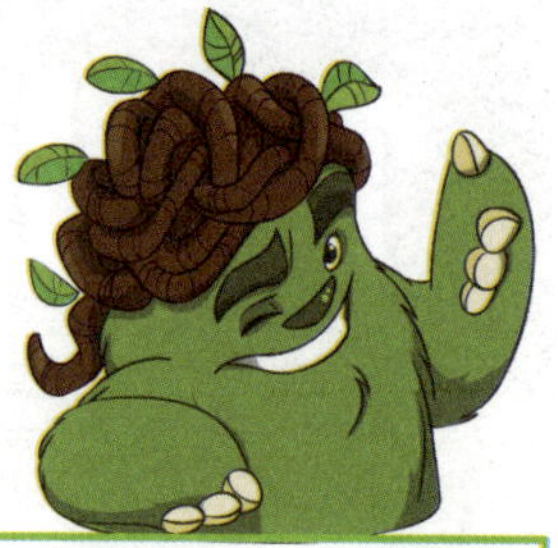

Hello, teacher!

Hello, teacher! What is this?
It's a pencil. Let's draw, please!

Repeat with: table, chair, book, crayon

❀ Optional: Draw your teacher.

 teacher, table, chair, book, crayon, pencil

Name

Lesson 2

❋ Classroom tour.

❋ Game: *Roll and say.*

❋ Play the story.  CD 1 • 14

❋ **WORKSHEET 2**: Say and match.

❋ Optional: Photocopiable 1: Trace.

❋ Optional: Colour.

What's this? It's a (book). It's (red).

Name

Lesson 3

- Game: *Happy and sad march.*
- Plasticine happy and sad faces.
- Play the story.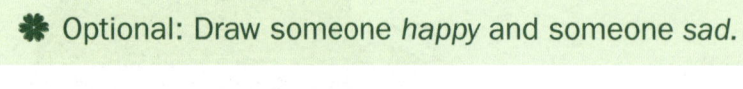
- Pop-out activity.
- **WORKSHEET 3**: Say *happy* or *sad*.
- Optional: Photocopiable 2: Paint and stick leaves on the tree.

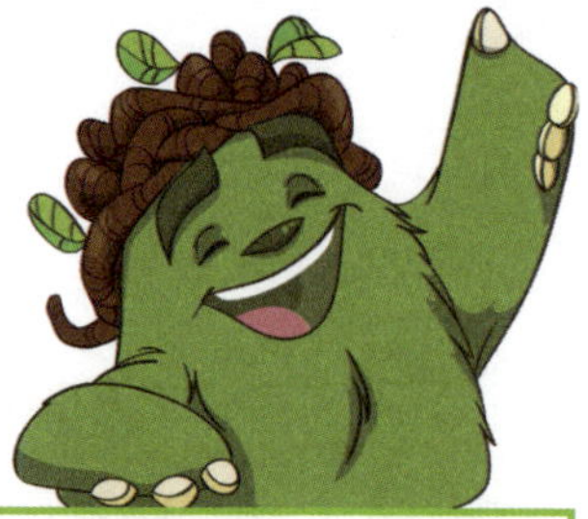

- Optional: Draw someone *happy* and someone *sad*.

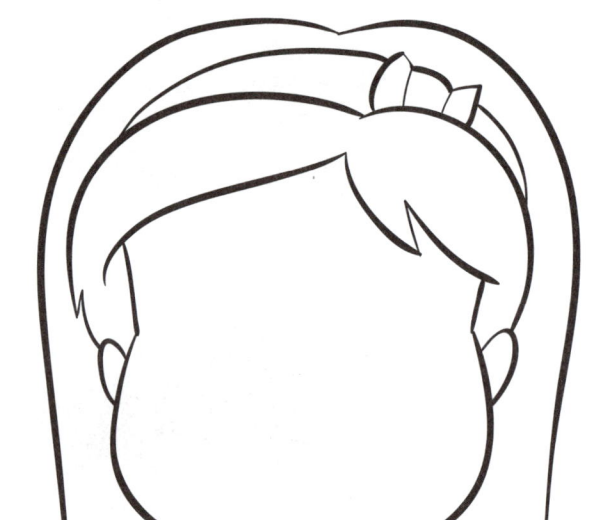

happy / sad

Name

15

Lesson 4

- Game: *Mime the word.*
- *Hello, everybody!* action song: Sing and do the actions.
- **WORKSHEET** 4 : Listen to the song and point.

Hello, everybody!

*Hello, everybody, what's your name?
I'm Sam. This is my chair.
I sit on my chair. I sit on my chair.
I sit on my chair like this!*

Repeat with:
Nico / play on my table
Sam / draw with my pencil
Nico / colour with my crayon
Sam / read my book
teacher / point at the circle

- Optional: Colour the ball red.

**teacher, table, chair, book, crayon, pencil
circle**

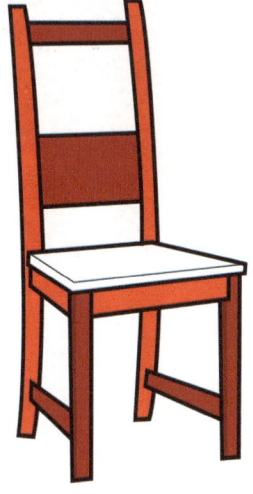

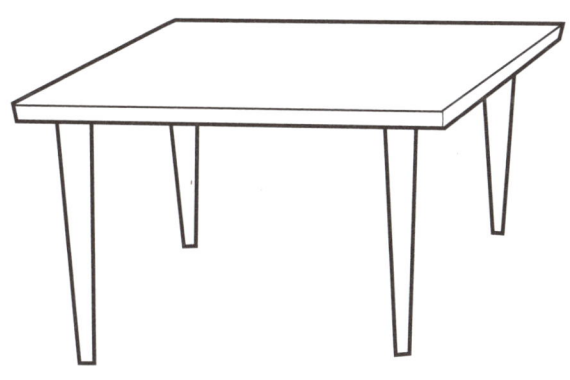

Name

Lesson 5

❦ Game: *Find red.*

❦ *I like red* song: Sing and point.

❦ **WORKSHEET 5**: Listen to the song and point. Then colour.

❦ Optional: Photocopiable 3: Trace the circles.

❦ Optional: Colour the circles red.

I like red

Red, red, I like red.
What's this? A red circle!
I like red!

Repeat with:
crayon, book, chair, table, teacher

teacher, table, chair, book, crayon, pencil circle, red

Consolidation

🍀 WORKSHEET 6

Name

19

EXTRA

Phonics Lesson

1 Listen and say the **s** letter sound.

2 Sing the song.

Say hello to Stella!

Hello, Stella!
Hello, Stella!
sssss I'm Stella!
sssss I'm Stella!

Hello, Stella!
Hello, Stella!
sssss I'm Stella, hello!
sssss

3 Listen, point and say the **s** words.

 Optional: Photocopiable 4: Colour Stella and the sun.

2 Let's Play!

Name

Lesson 1

- Pass the cards.
- *My toys* song: Sing and point.
- **WORKSHEET 1**: Say and colour.

My toys

My toys, my toys. Let's play!
Lots of toys. Hooray!

A ball, a ball. Let's play!
A ball, a ball. Hooray!

Repeat with:
teddy, doll, train, bike, car

- Optional: Colour the toys.

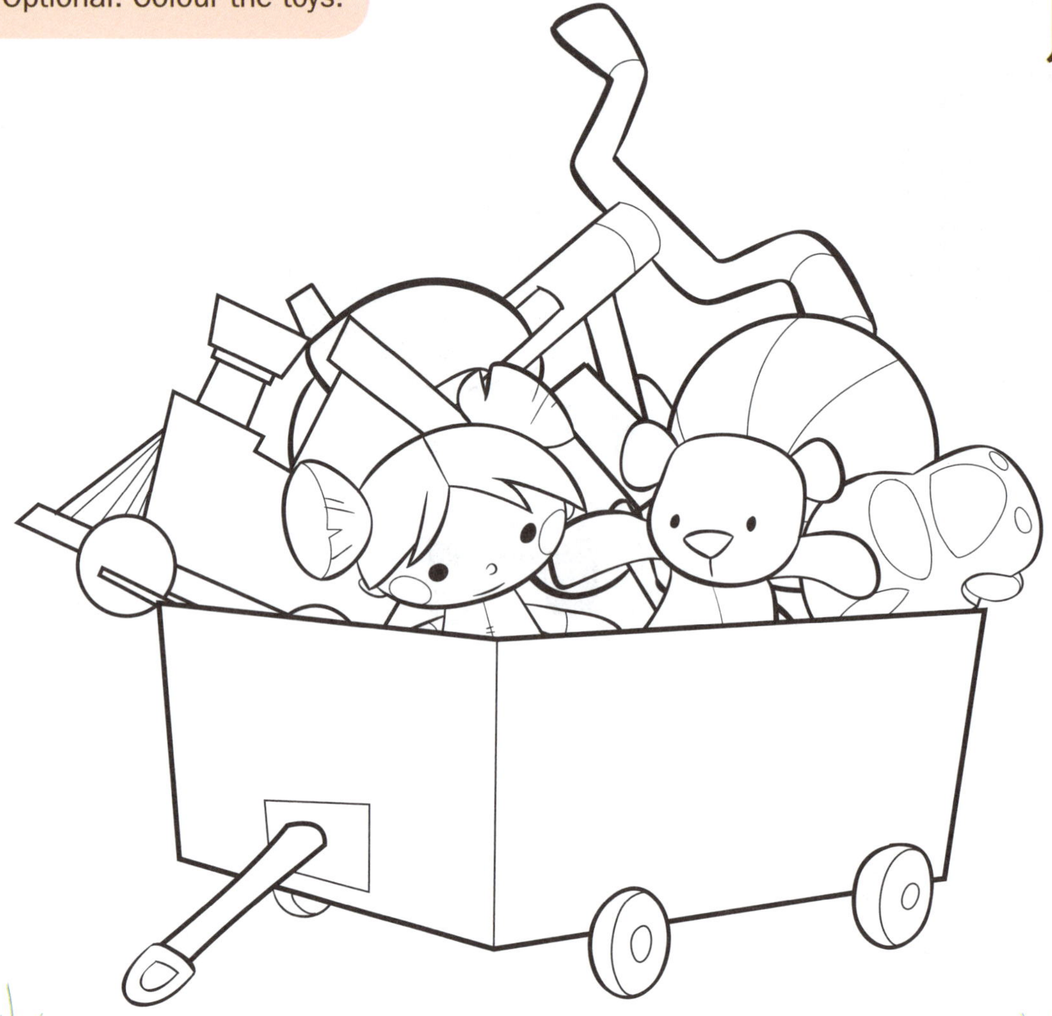

 **ball, teddy, doll, train, bike, car**

Name

23

Lesson 2

- There's a train.
- Here you are.
- Play the story. CD 1 22
- **WORKSHEET 2**: Say, match and colour.
- Optional: Photocopiable 5: Find and colour the different toy.

- Optional: Colour.

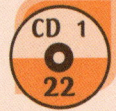

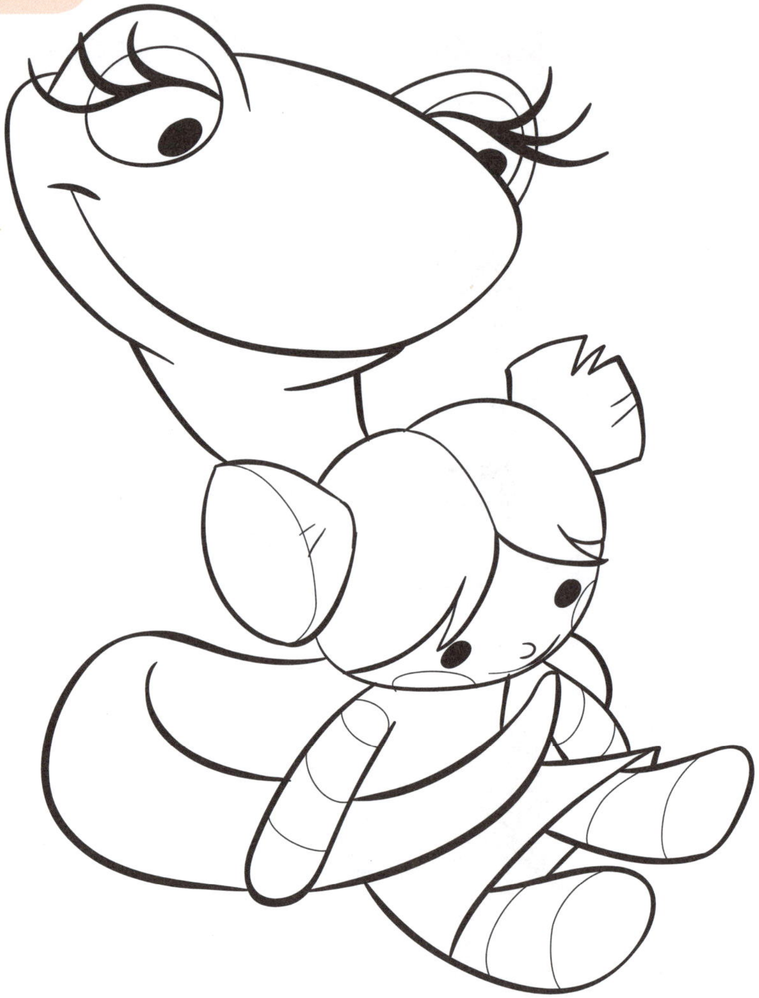

There's one (red) (car). Here you are. / Thank you.
red, blue

Name

Lesson 3

- Fast and slow.
- Play the story. CD 1 / 22
- Pop-out activity.
- **WORKSHEET 3**: Say *fast* or *slow*.
- Optional: Photocopiable 6: Find and circle the four differences.

- Optional: Colour *fast* and *slow*.

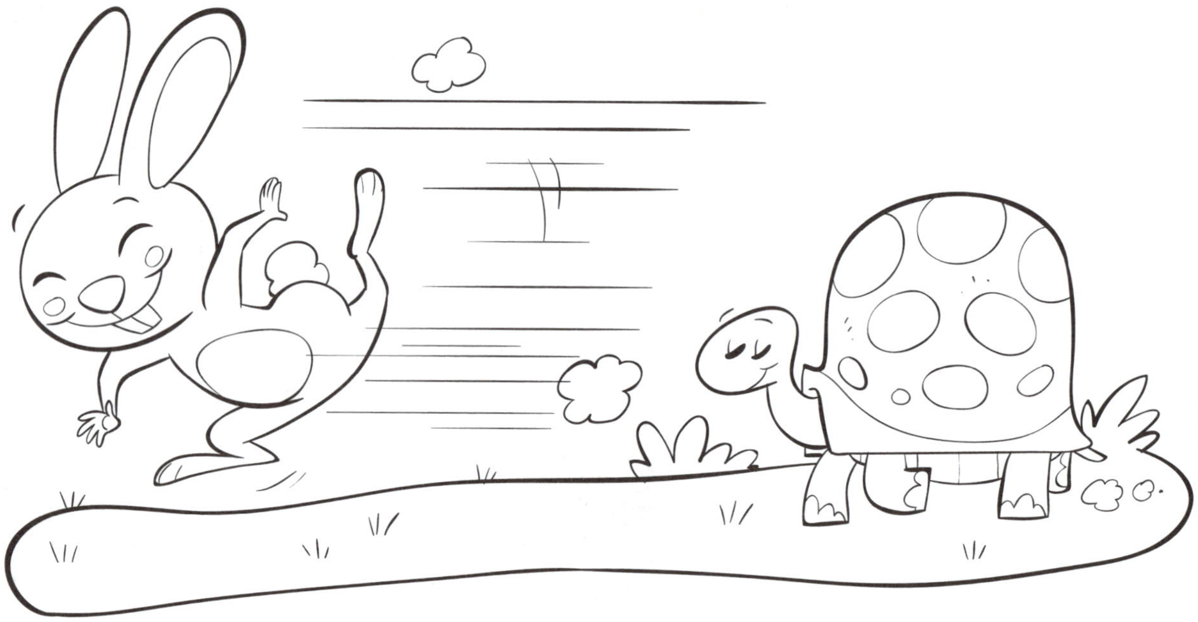

Name

Lesson 4

- Game: *Pass and say.*

- *Look at my toys* action song: Sing and do the actions.

- **Worksheet 4**: Listen to the song, point and colour.

Look at my toys

Look at my toys. Look at me.
There's one ball. Play with me!

Bounce the ball slow, slow, slow.
Bounce the ball fast, fast, fast!
Stop!

Repeat with: move the train, ride the bike, move the car

Play with me!

- Optional: Colour the ball blue.

ball, train, bike, car
fast / slow

Name

29

Lesson 5

- Plasticine number 1.
- *One happy rabbit* number song: Sing and count.
- **WORKSHEET 5**: Trace, count and colour.
- Optional: Photocopiable 7: Trace number 1. Then colour.

One happy rabbit

There's one happy rabbit on one chair.

There's one happy rabbit. Come on, let's play!

Teddy bear, teddy bear, you're so blue.
Teddy bear, teddy bear, I love you!

- Optional: Draw your favourite toy.

 blue
one

Consolidation

WORKSHEET 6

Name

31

EXTRA

Phonics Lesson

1 Listen and say the **g** and **b** letter sounds.

32

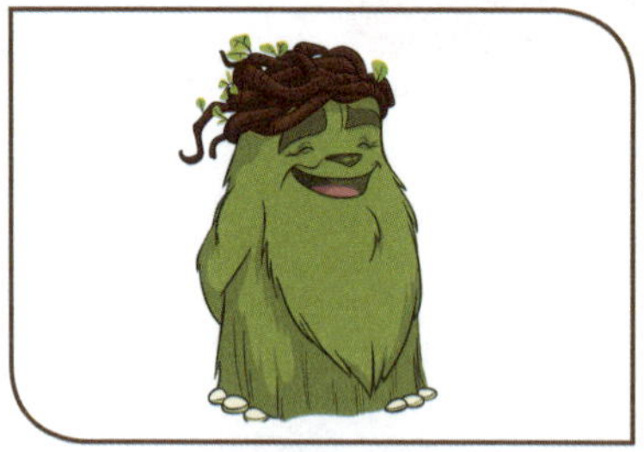

2 Sing the song.

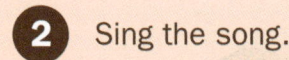

g – g – g   I'm Greenman!
g – g – g   I'm Greenman!
g – g – g   I'm green!
I'm Greenman!

g – g – g   Greenman!
I'm green.
I'm Greenman!

3 Sing the song.

b – b – b   This is my book.
My big, blue book!
b – b – b   This is my book.
My big, blue book!

Optional: Photocopiable 8: Make a book of **b** words.

Autumn Fun!

Name

33

Autumn Fun!

♣ Autumn weather.

♣ *It's autumn* song.

♣ **WORKSHEET 1**: Say and match.

♣ Optional: Photocopiables 9 and 10: Draw, colour, cut and stick to make an autumn scene.

CD 1 • 28

It's autumn

It's autumn in the magic forest.
It's autumn in the magic forest.

The sky is blue, the leaves are red.
I'm happy, I'm happy it's autumn time.

I'm happy, I'm happy it's autumn time.

♣ Optional: Colour the crayons blue and red.

teacher, table, chair, book, crayon, pencil, ball, teddy, doll, train, bike, car

3 The Big Monster

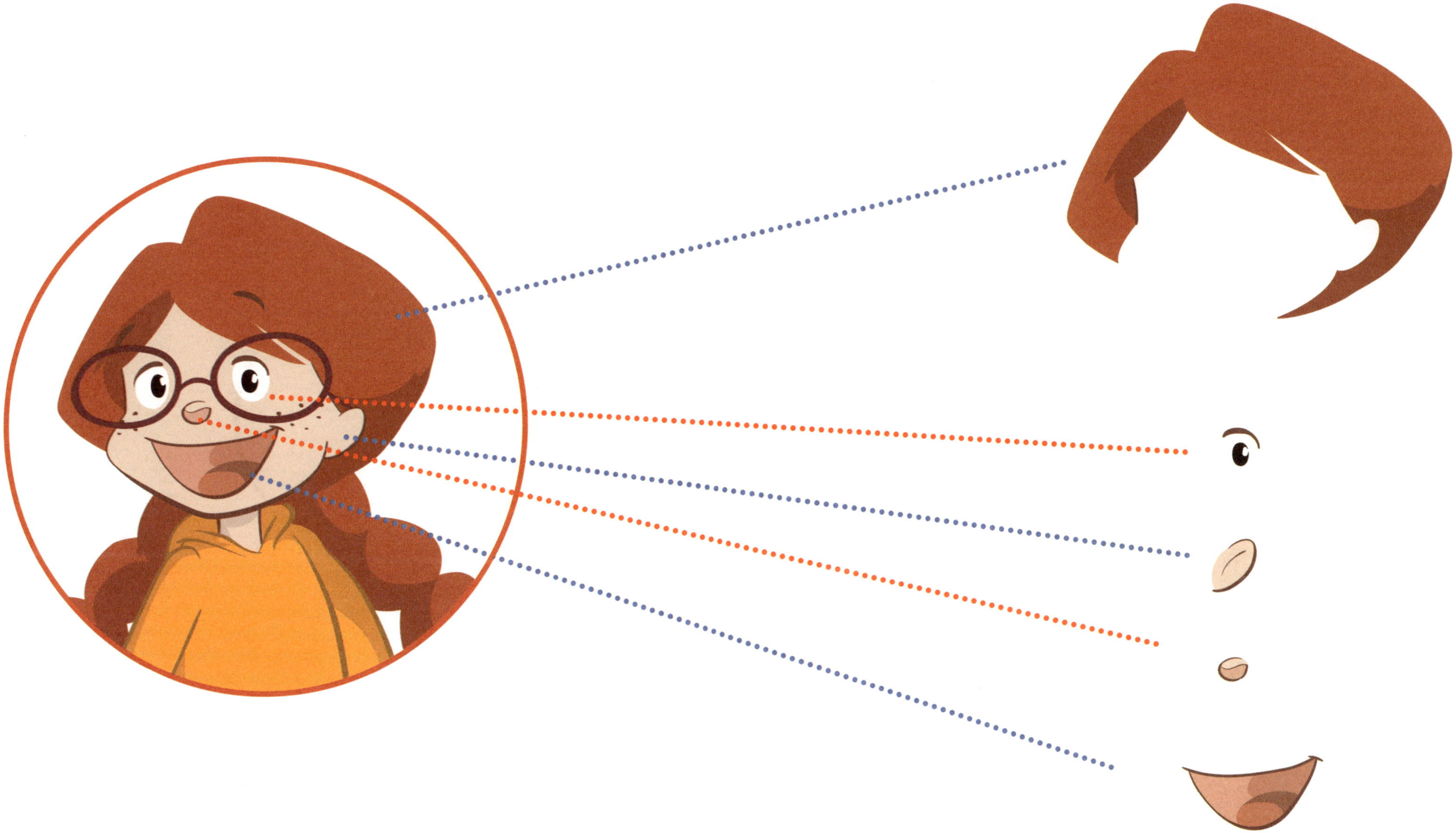

Name

35

Lesson 1

- Show, touch and repeat.
- *Touch your face* song: Sing and touch.
- **WORKSHEET 1**: Trace blue or red and say.

CD 1 30

Touch your face

Touch your face, face, face.
Touch your nose, nose, nose.
Touch your eye, eye, eye.
Touch your hair, hair, hair.
Touch your ear, ear, ear.
Touch your mouth, mouth, mouth!

Touch your face!

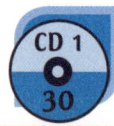

Optional: Draw a happy face.

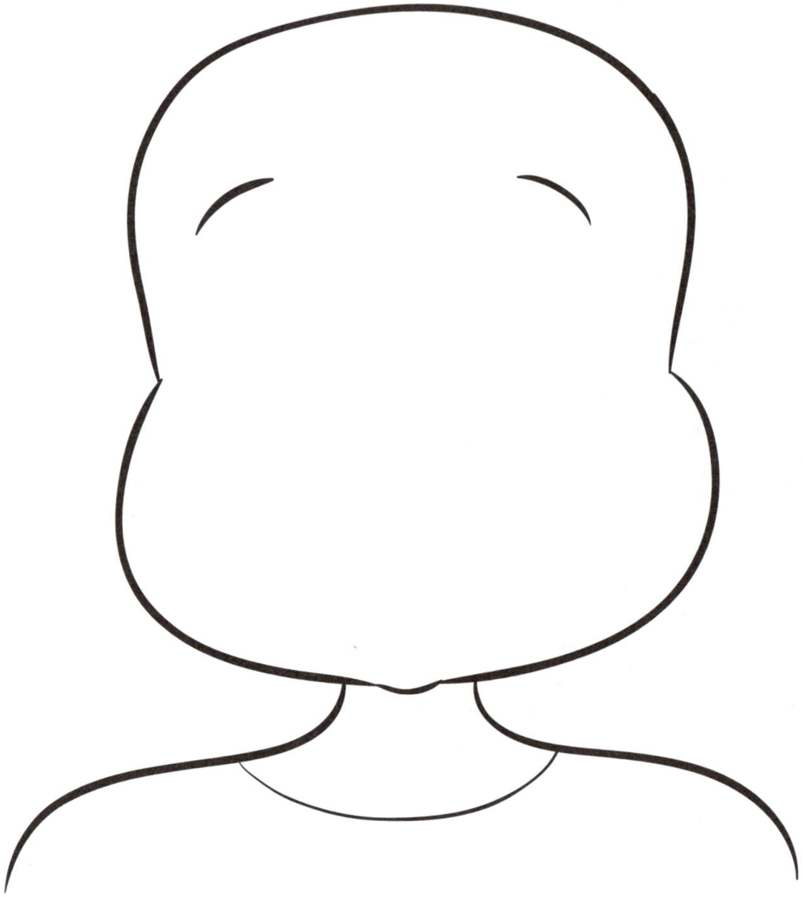

CD 1 29

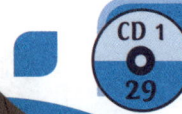

face, eye, ear, mouth, nose, hair

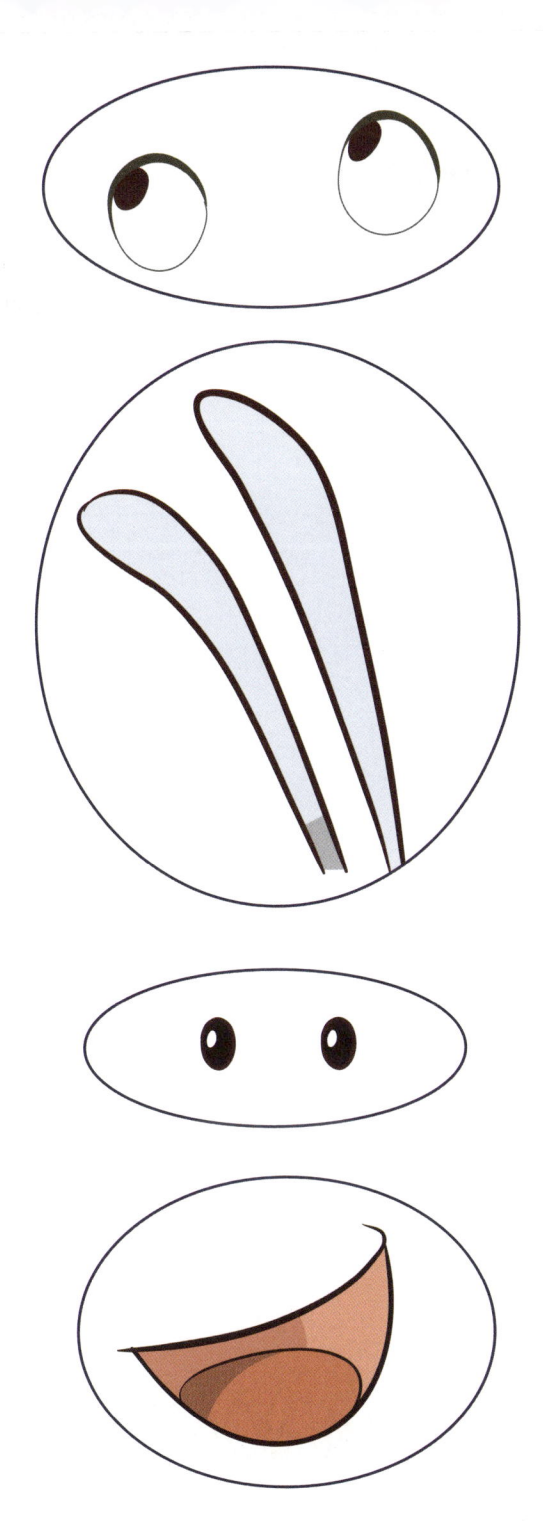

Name

37

Lesson 2

- Pass the ball.
- Touch your head.
- Play the story. (CD 1, 31)
- **WORKSHEET 2**: Say *big* or *small* and match.
- Optional: Photocopiable 11: Draw what comes next: *big* or *small*?

- Optional: Draw your face.

I can see (one) (big) nose. / It's got (two) (small) ears.

Name

39

Lesson 3

- I'm small!
- Big and small objects.
- Play the story. CD 1 · 31
- Pop-out activity.
- **WORKSHEET** 3: Say *big* or *small* and colour.
- Optional: Photocopiable 12: Draw a monster face.

Optional: Colour *big* and *small*.

big / small

Name

41

Lesson 4

- Look and say.
- *This is my face* action song: Sing and do the actions.
- **WORKSHEET** 4: Listen to the song, point and colour.

This is my face

Hello, everybody!
This is my face.

I've got one big mouth.
One big mouth!

I've got two big ears.
Two big ears!

I've got one big nose.
One big nose!

I've got two big eyes.
Two big eyes!

On my face!

Repeat with: *small*

Optional: Colour the faces.

face, eye, ear, mouth, nose
big / small

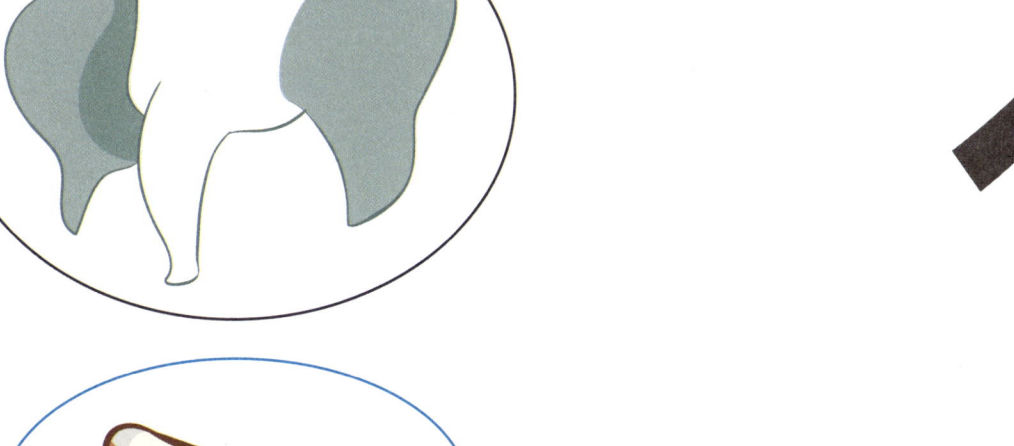

Name

43

Lesson 5

- Game: *Find the number.*
- *One, two* song: Sing and count.
- **WORKSHEET 5**: Count and match.
- Optional: Photocopiable 13: Look, count and trace 1 or 2.

CD 1 · 33

One, two

One, two. One, two.
Can you count one and two?
One, two. One, two.
Peek-a-boo, I see you!

I can see two eyes.
One! Two!
I can see two ears.
One! Two!

One, two. One, two.
Can you count one and two?
One, two. One, two.
Peek-a-boo, I see you!

Optional: Colour the faces.

numbers 1 - 2
green

Consolidation

WORKSHEET 6

Name

45

EXTRA

Phonics Lesson

1 Listen and say the **n** and **m** letter sounds.

CD 1 · 34

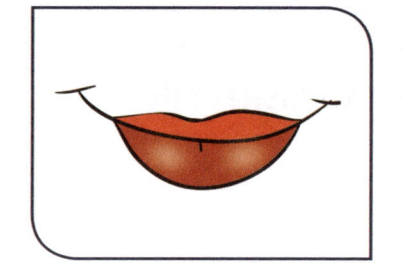

2 Sing the song.

CD 1 · 35

n – n – n   I'm Nico.
n – n – n   This is my nose!
n – n – n   I'm Nico.
And this is my nose!
This is my nose!
n – n – n

3 Sing the song.

CD 1 · 36

m – m – m   This is my mouth.
mmmmm   My mouth!
m – m – m   This is my mouth.
mmmmm   My mouth!

🌱 Optional: Photocopiable 14: Draw a mouth and a nose on Nico.

46

4 My Family

Name

47

Lesson 1

🍁 Help Greenman pass the cards.

🍁 *My family* song: Listen and sing.

🍁 **WORKSHEET 1**: Say and colour.

🍁 Optional: Draw your family.

My family

Hello, hello. Come with me.
This is my family.

Hello, mummy, how are you?
Hello, mummy, I love you!

Hello, hello. Come with me.
This is my family.

Repeat with:
daddy, brother, sister, baby, friend

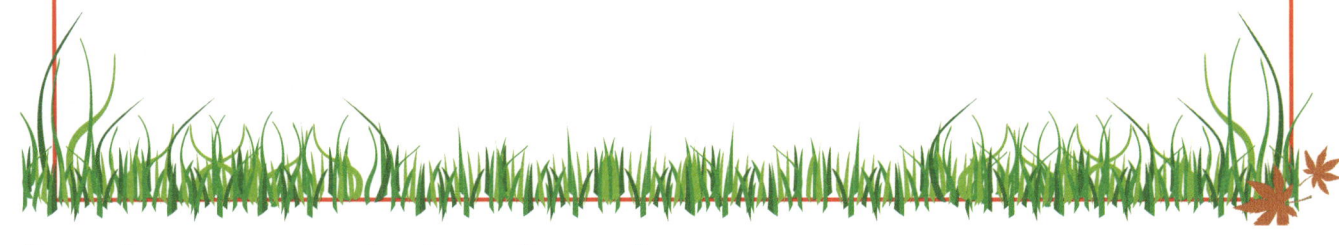

mummy, daddy, brother, sister, baby, friend

Name

49

Lesson 2

- Game: *Can I have?*
- Play the story. (CD 2, 03)
- **WORKSHEET 2**: Say and circle *green* or *red*.
- Optional: Photocopiable 15: Look and match.

- Optional: Colour the baby.

Who is it? It's (Sam's) (brother). / They've got (red) (hair).

Name

51

Lesson 3

- Same or different?
- Game: *Pass and say.*
- Play the story. CD 2 03
- Pop-out activity.
- **WORKSHEET 3:** Say *same* or *different* and match.
- Optional: Photocopiable 16: Find and circle the three differences.

- Optional: Colour the family.

same / different

Name

53

Lesson 4

- Game: Who's missing?
- Who is it? action song: Sing and do the actions
- **WORKSHEET 4**: Listen to the song, point and colour.

Who is it?

Who is it? Who is it?
It's my mummy.
She's got red hair.
I've got red hair.
We look the same!

Who is it? Who is it?
It's my daddy.
He's got a small nose.
I've got a small nose.
We look the same!

Who is it? Who is it?
It's my baby brother.
He's got big eyes.
I've got big eyes.
We look the same!

Who is it? Who is it?
It's my sister.
She's got a small mouth.
I've got a small mouth.
We look the same!

Who is it? Who is it?
It's my friend.
He's got big ears.
I've got small ears.
We look different!

- Optional: Draw your best friend.

**mummy, daddy, brother, sister, baby, friend
same / different**

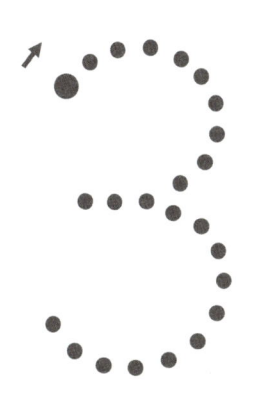

1
2
3

Name

55

Lesson 5

- Walk on the numbers.

- *Can you count to 3?* number song 1–3: Sing and count.

- **WORKSHEET 5**: Trace and count. Then, match and colour.

- Optional: Photocopiable 17: Trace and make a family triangle.

CD 2 · 05

Can you count to 3?

1, 2, 3.
Can you see?
Can you count to 3 with me?
One, two, three!

1, 2, 3.
Can you see?
Can you count 3 fingers with me?
One, two, three!

1, 2, 3.
Can you see?
Can you draw a triangle with me?
One, two, three!

1, 2, 3.
Can you see?
You can count to 3 with me!
One, two, three!

- Optional: Trace and colour.

**numbers 1 - 3
triangle, yellow**

Consolidation

WORKSHEET 6

Name

57

EXTRA

Phonics Lesson

1 Listen and say the **f** and **u** letter sounds.

2 Sing the song.

f - f - f   I'm Frog.
In the forest!

And this is my family.
In the forest!

We're the forest frog family!
f - f - f

3 Sing the song.

u – u – u   Umbrella!
u – u – u   Umbrella!
u – u – u   Under the umbrella!

Optional: Photocopiable 18: Trace the umbrella and colour the frogs.

58

Winter Fun!

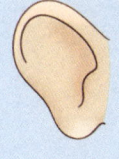

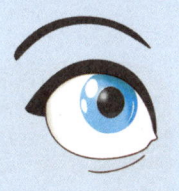

Name _____   59

Winter Fun!

❄ Winter weather.

❄ Same or different.

❄ *It's wintertime* song.

❄ **Worksheet 1**: Say and match.

❄ Optional: Photocopiables 19 and 20:
Trace and make a windy cloud.
Make a snowman family.

❄ Optional: Trace and colour.

It's wintertime

It's wintertime. Let's go!
It's wintertime. Let's go,
It's wintertime. Let's go!
It's very cold in the forest today.

Repeat with: windy, snowy

**face, eye, ear, mouth, nose, hair
mummy, daddy, brother, sister, baby, friend**

5 Where's My Bird?

Name

61

Lesson 1

- Pass the cards with Greenman.
- Game: *Give me the hamster.*
- *I've got a bird* song: Listen and sing.
- **WORKSHEET 1**: Say the animal and colour.

- Optional: Draw your favourite pet.

I've got a bird

*I've got a bird, a hamster and a fish.
I've got a dog, a turtle and a cat.*

*I've got a bird. A blue, blue bird!
I've got a hamster.
A yellow, yellow hamster!
I've got a fish. A red, red fish!
I've got a turtle. A green, green turtle!
I've got a dog. A yellow, yellow dog!
I've got a cat. A blue, blue cat!*

*I've got a bird, a hamster and a fish.
I've got a dog, a turtle and a cat.*

turtle, fish, bird, hamster, cat, dog

Name

63

Lesson 2

- Guess my pet.
- Role play.
- Play the story. CD 2 / 12
- **WORKSHEET 2**: Say the animal. Then say *on* or *under* and match.
- Optional: Photocopiable 21: Find and circle the pets. Then colour.

- Optional: Colour the animals.

Can you see your (bird)? It's (on) the (table). / The (cat) is (under) the (chair).

Name

65

Lesson 3

- Game: *Walk to the word.*
- Where's the pencil?
- Play the story. **CD 2 · 12**
- Pop-out activity.
- **WORKSHEET 3**: Colour *on* or *under*.
- Optional: Photocopiable 22: Help Nico find the bird.

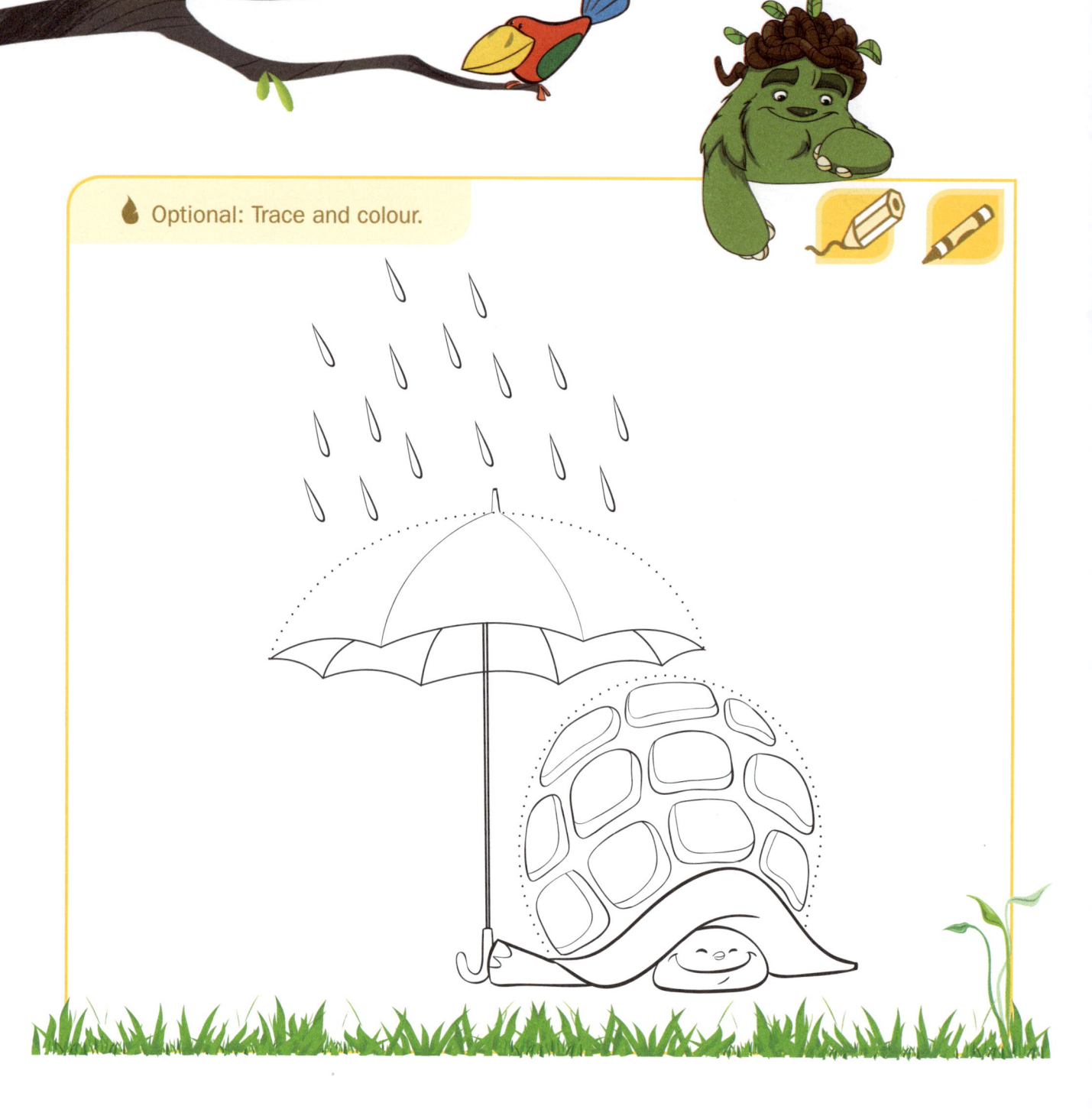

- Optional: Trace and colour.

on / under

Name

67

Lesson 4

- Say the animal.
- *On, under* action song: Sing and do the actions.
- **WORKSHEET 4**: Listen to the song, point and colour.

- Optional: Trace and colour.

On, under

On, under! On, under!
Can you see?

My dog is on the table.
Hee, hee, hee!

On, under! On, under!
Can you see?

My cat is under the chair.
My dog is on the table.
Hee, hee, hee!

Add on:
hamster: on the ball, fish: under the table, bird: on my nose, turtle: under the book

**turtle, fish, bird, hamster, cat, dog
on / under**

2

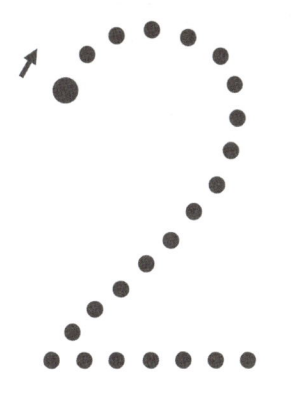

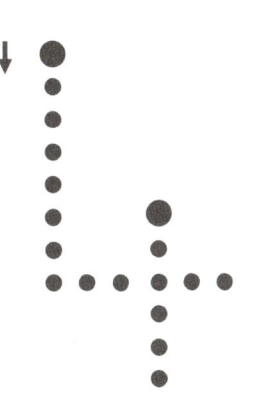

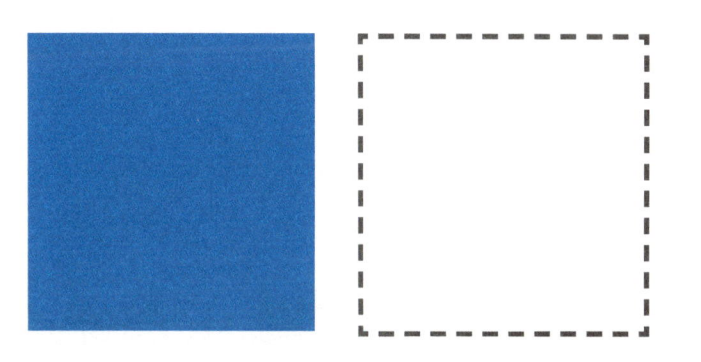

3

4

Name

Lesson 5

- Say the number.

- *Can you count to 4? number song 1-4*: Sing and count.

- **WORKSHEET 5**: Trace and count. Then, match and colour.

- Optional: Photocopiable 23: Trace the shapes.

CD 2 · 14

Can you count to 4?

1, 2, 3, 4.
Can you see?
Can you count to 4 with me?
One, two, three, four!

1, 2, 3, 4.
Can you see?
Can you draw a square with me?
One, two, three, four!

1, 2, 3, 4.
Can you see?
Can you count four fingers with me?
One, two, three, four!

1, 2, 3, 4.
Can you see?
You can count to 4 with me!
One, two, three, four!

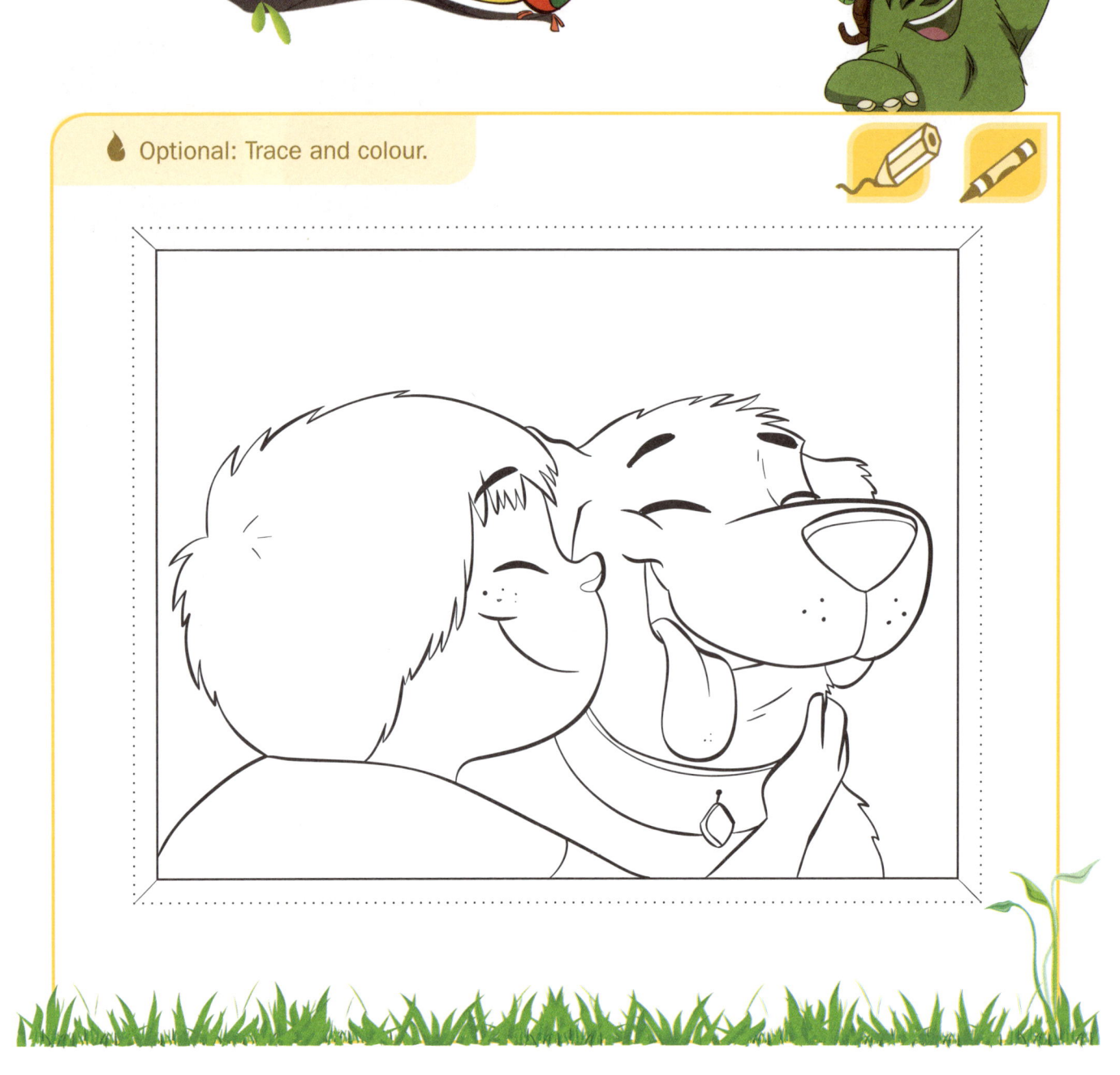

- Optional: Trace and colour.

numbers 1 - 4
square

Consolidation

WORKSHEET 6

Name

71

EXTRA
Phonics Lesson

1 Listen and say the **d** and **c/k** letter sounds.

CD 2 · 15

2 Sing the song.

CD 2 · 16

d – d – d – d – d – d – d – d
Hello, dog!
Hello, little dog!
What are you doing, little dog?
d – d – d – d – d – d – d – d
The dog is dancing!

3 Sing the song.

CD 2 · 17

c – c – c
Look! A cat!
A cat with a kitten!
And a kite!
A cat with a kitten and a kite!
k – k – k

Optional: Photocopiable 24: Make a kite.

6 Let's Tidy Up!

Name

73

Lesson 1

- I like cake!
- Give the card to Greenman.
- *The summer picnic* song: Sing and do the actions.
- **WORKSHEET 1:** Say and colour the food.

CD 2 · 19

The summer picnic

A picnic, a picnic.
Let's have a summer picnic!

Pasta, pasta, I like pasta!
Pasta, pasta. Let's have pasta!

Repeat with:
sandwiches, cake, apples, bananas, milk

- Optional: Draw your favourite food for a picnic.

CD 2 · 18

sandwich, cake, pasta, apple, banana, milk

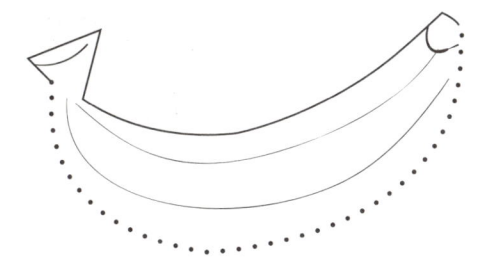

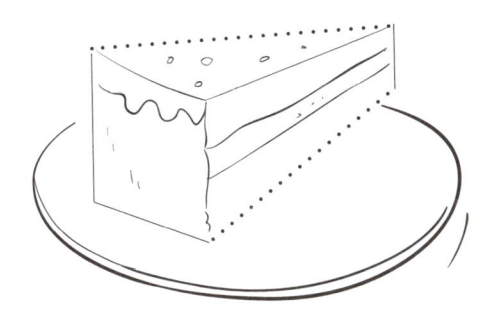

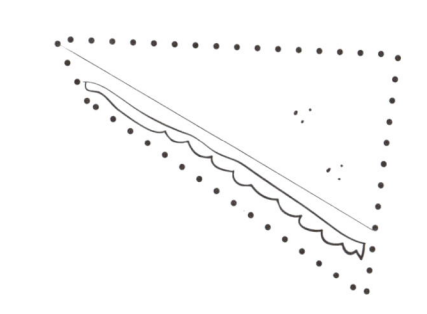

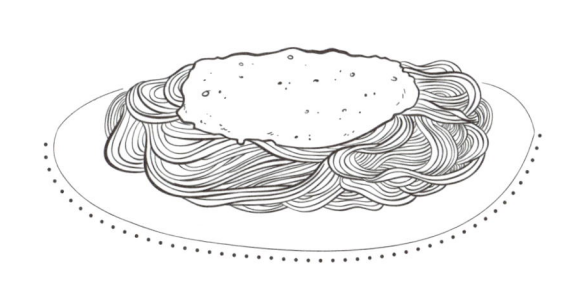

Name

75

Lesson 2

🍃 I like…!

🍃 Game: *The hoop game.*

🍃 Play the story. **CD 2 / 20**

🍃 **WORKSHEET 2**: Trace, say and colour.

🍃 Optional: Photocopiable 25: Draw what comes next.

🍃 Optional: Trace and colour.

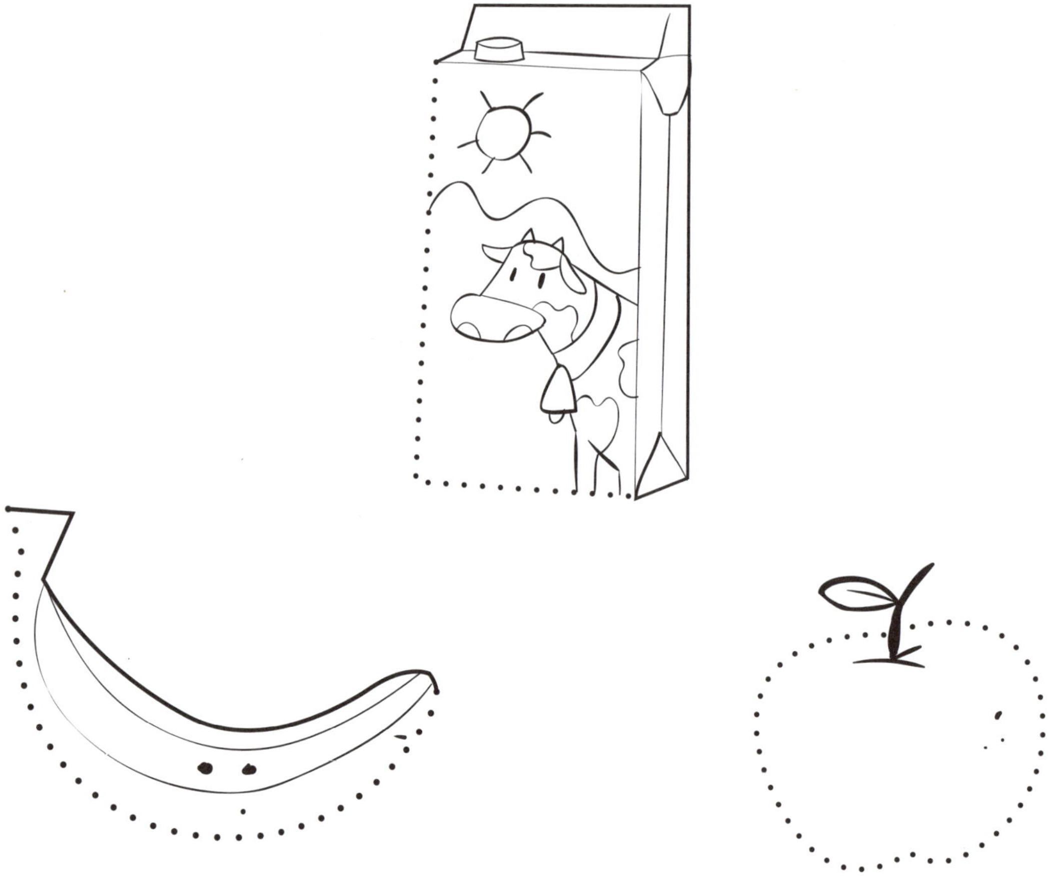

I like (bananas). / Let's (eat).

Name

77

Lesson 3

- Tidy up!
- Play the story. CD 2 • 20
- Pop-out activity.
- **WORKSHEET 3**: Say *tidy* or *messy* and find the 4 differences.
- Optional: Photocopiable 26: Look and match. Then colour.

- Optional: Trace and colour the tidy room.

tidy / messy

Name

79

Lesson 4

- Listen and move.
- *I like summer* action song: Sing and do the actions.
- **WORKSHEET 4**: Say and match.

- Optional: Trace and colour.

I like summer

I like summer. Hooray, hooray!
I like summer. Hooray, hooray!
Let's have a picnic.
It's a lovely day!

Let's make a sandwich!
Let's make a sandwich!
Let's make a sandwich.
It's a lovely day!

Repeat with:
eat apples and bananas, drink milk,
eat spaghetti, make a cake

sandwich, cake, pasta, apple, banana, milk

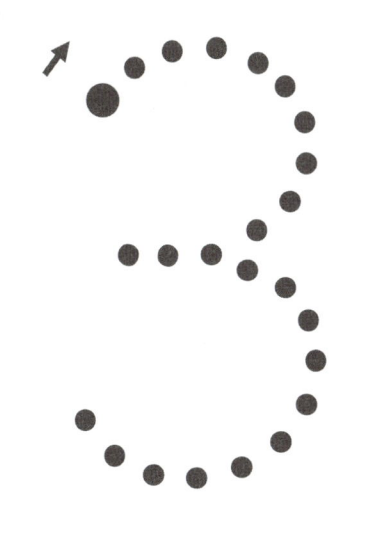

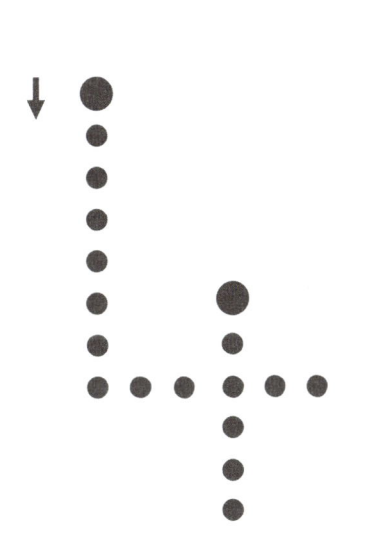

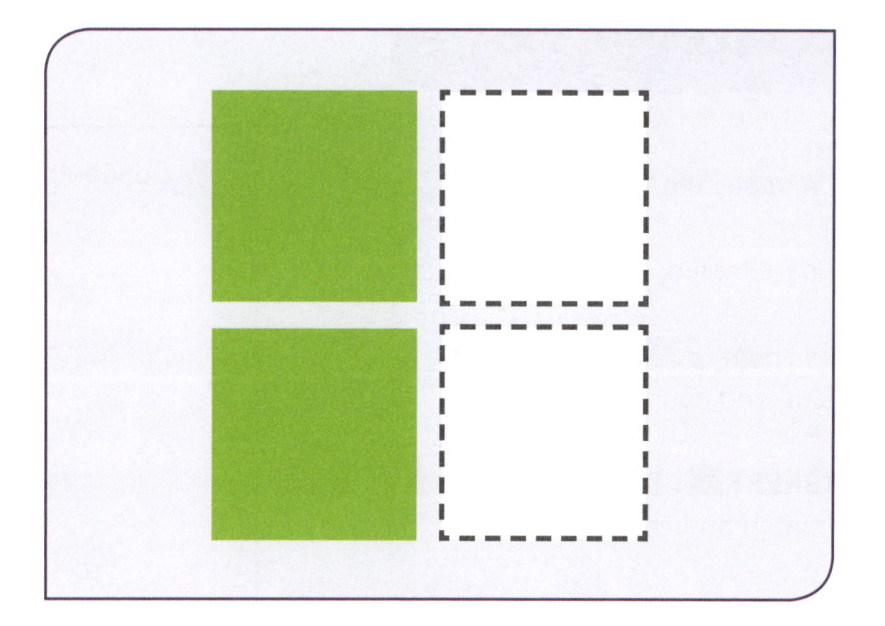

Name

Lesson 5

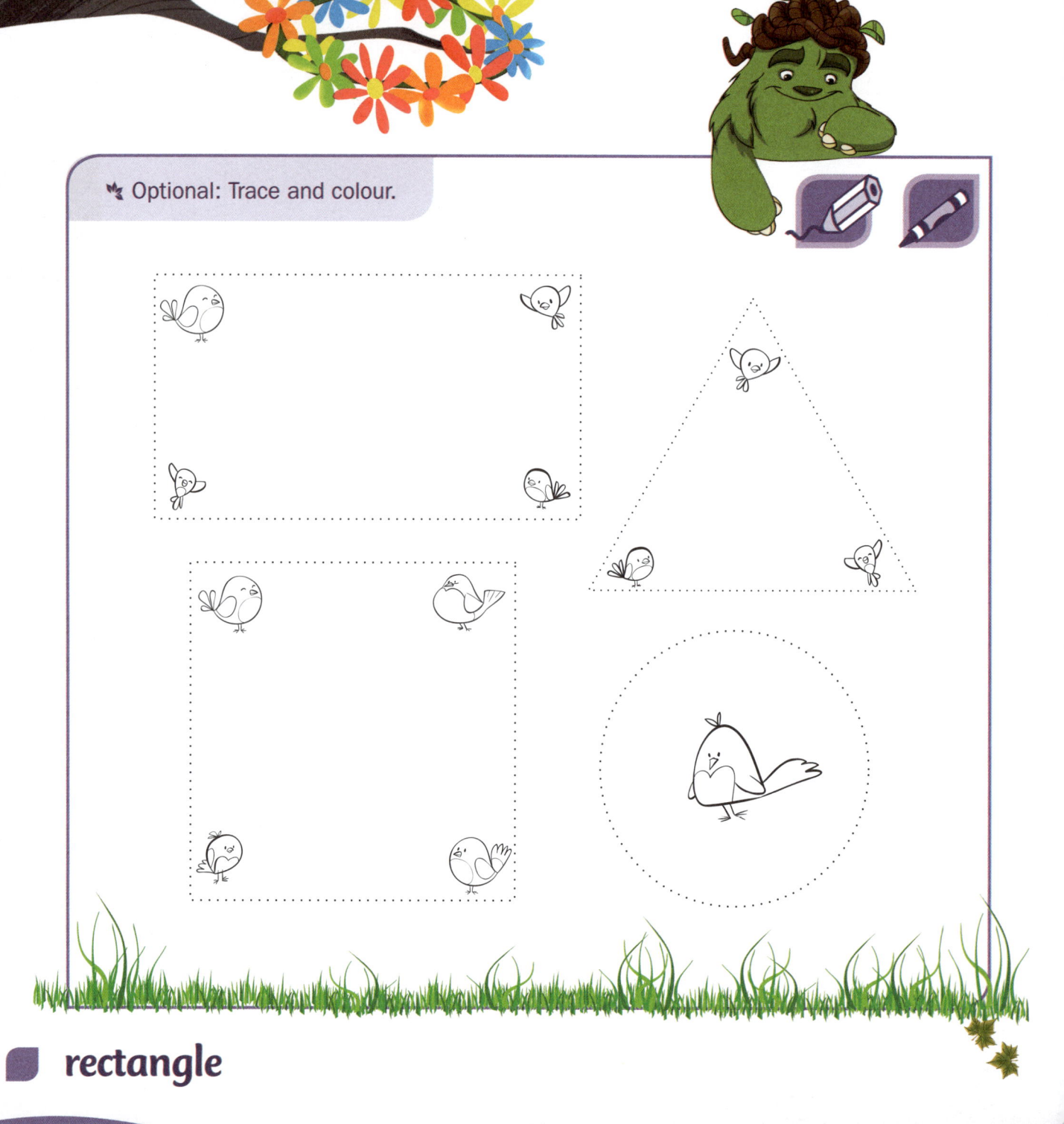

- Listen and say the number.

- Pick the rectangle.

- You can count to 4! number song 1–4: Sing and count.

- **WORKSHEET 5:** Trace and count. Then, match and colour.

- Optional: Photocopiable 27: Look and match.

CD 2
22

You can count to 4!

1, 2, 3.
Can you see?
Can you draw a triangle with me?
One, two, three!

1, 2, 3, 4.
Can you see?
Can you draw a square with me?
One, two, three, four!

1, 2, 3, 4.
Can you see?
Can you draw a rectangle with me?
One, two, three, four!
1, 2, 3, 4.

1, 2, 3, 4.
Can you see?
You can count to 4 with me!
One, two, three, four!

- Optional: Trace and colour.

rectangle

Consolidation

WORKSHEET 6

Name

83

84

EXTRA

Phonics Lesson

1 Listen and say the **p** letter sound.

CD 2 · 23

2 Sing the song.

CD 2 · 24

p – p – p   I like pasta!
p – p – p   I like pizza!
Pizza and pasta, please!

p – p – p   I like pasta!
p – p – p   I like pizza!
Pizza and pasta, please!

3 Listen, point and say the **p** words.

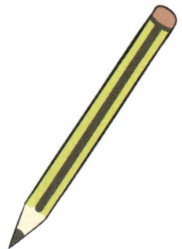

CD 2 · 25

🌸 Optional: Photocopiable 28: Make pasta cards.

Spring Fun!

Name _____

85

Spring Fun!

✿ Spring weather.

✿ Say the vocabulary.

✿ Guess the animal.

✿ Sing for spring! song.

✿ **WORKSHEET 1**: Say and match.

✿ Optional: Photocopiables 29 and 30: Colour, cut and stick to make a spring scene.

CD2 26

Sing for spring!

Can you see the butterfly?
Can you see the sunny sky?
Can you hear the forest sing… for spring?

Let's sing!
For spring!

Sing for spring!
Sing for spring!

✿ Optional: Trace and colour.

turtle, fish, bird, hamster, cat, dog, sandwich, cake, pasta, apple, banana, milk

Halloween

cat, monster, pumpkin

Name

87

★ Optional: Photocopiable 34: Make a pumpkin mobile.

Phonics

1 Listen and say the **h** and **a** letter sounds.

CD 2 · 29

2 Sing the song.

CD 2 · 30

h – h – h
Hello!
h – h – h
I'm Hedgehog!
h – h – h
I'm happy!
Happy Halloween!
Happy Halloween!

3 Sing the song.

CD 2 · 31

a – a – a   Apple!
a – a – a   An apple!
a – a – a   Ants!
Ants on the apple!

★ Optional: Photocopiable 35: Make a happy hedgehog mask.

Christmas

MERRY CHRISTMAS

Christmas, tree, toy

Name

89

❄ Optional: Photocopiable 36: Make a Christmas tree.

Phonics

1 Listen and say the **r** letter sound.

CD 2 · 34

2 Sing the song.

CD 2 · 35

r r r r r
Here's Rabbit!
r r r r r
Run, Rabbit, run!
r r r r r
Rabbit's running with the reindeers!

It's Christmas!
Happy Christmas, everyone!

3 Say the **r** words.

❄ Optional: Photocopiable 37: Make a Christmas card.

Easter Carnival

Easter egg, bunny, chocolate

Name

Optional: Photocopiable 38: Make an Easter Bunny.

91

Phonics

1 Listen and say the *e* letter sound.

CD 2 · 38

2 Sing the song.

CD 2 · 39

e – e – e
Eggs in a nest.
A red egg,
A blue egg.
And a yellow egg.

e – e – e
Eggs in a nest!

3 Say he *e* words.

❖ Optional: Photocopiable 39: Make Easter eggs.

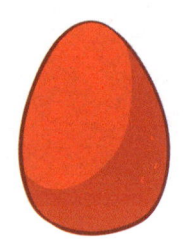

Green Day

forest, flower, beautiful

Name

Optional: Photocopiable 40: Make a tree for the forest.

93

Summer Fun!

* Go to the flashcard.
* Color hunt.
* *Family fun* song.
* **WORKSHEET 1**: Say and match.
* Optional: Photocopiables 31 and 32:
  Make a family chain.
  Trace and make a sun.

CD 2 — 44

Family fun

1, 2, 3, 4.

1, 2, 3, 4, family fun!
Playing in the summer sun!

1, 2, 3, 4, family fun!
I love summer time!

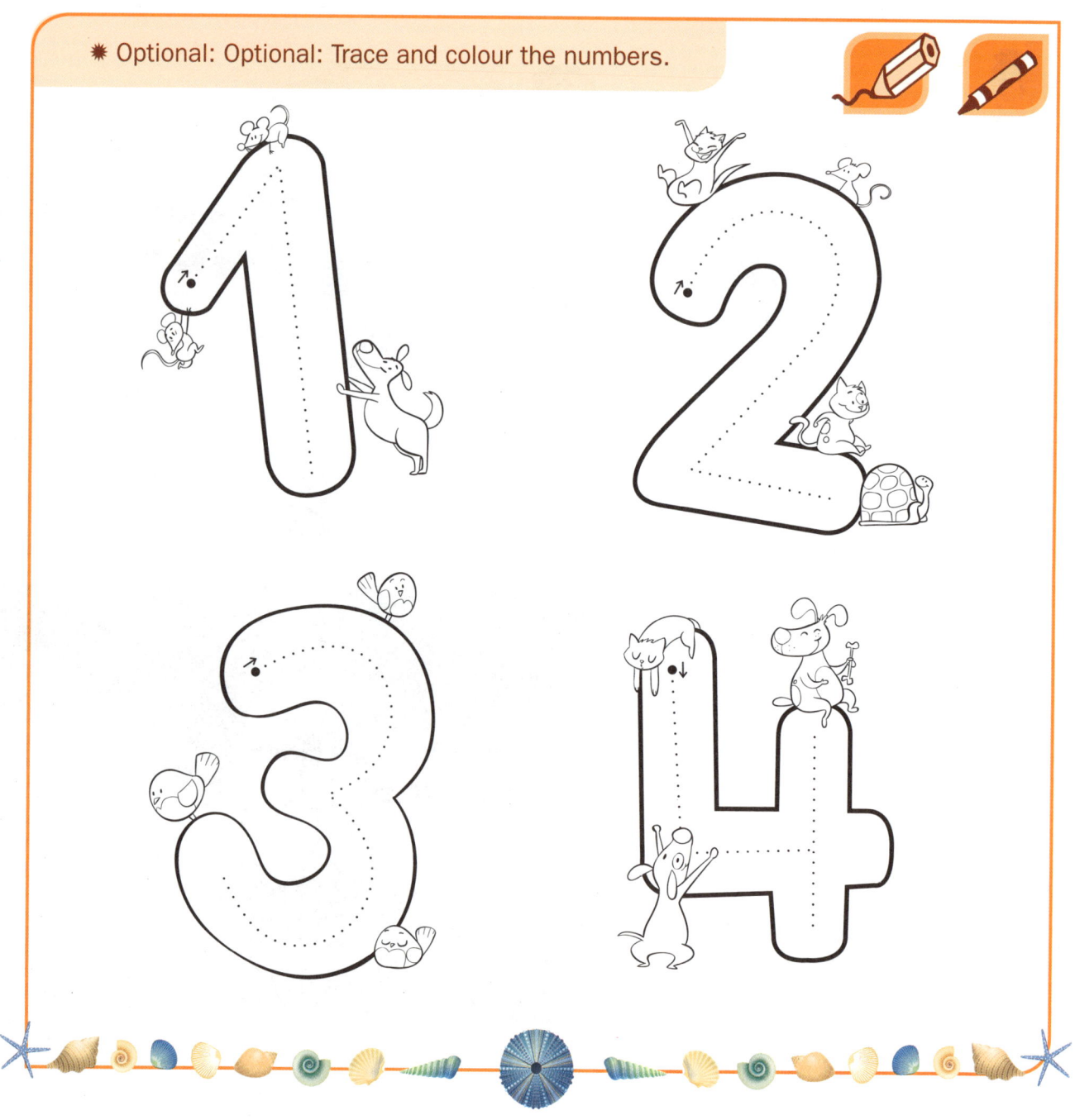

* Optional: Optional: Trace and colour the numbers.

teacher, pencil, bike, dog, friend, ball, bird, book, flower